# What Is She Playing?

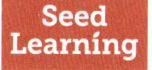
Seed Learning

# violin

# guitar

harmonica

piano

flute

trumpet

# harp

# drum

# What is she playing?

She is playing the violin.

# What is she playing?

She is playing the guitar.

# What is he playing?

# He is playing the harmonica.

# What is he playing?

He is playing
the piano.

# What is he playing?

# He is playing the flute.

# What is she playing?

She is playing the drum.

# Let's learn about the Philippines.

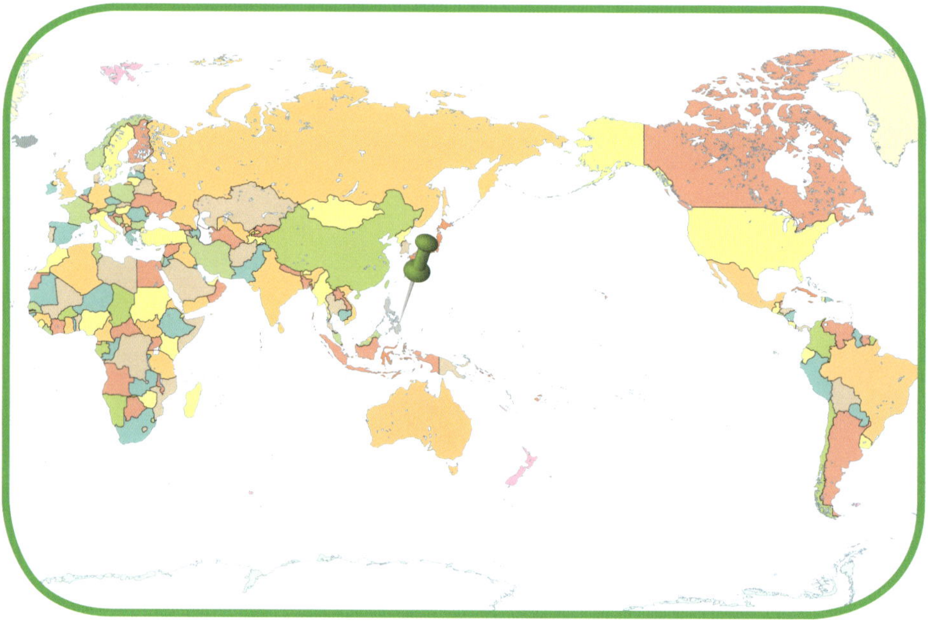

Flag of Philippines

Jeepney